Early Morning Revival Challenge

Books by Mrs. White

Mother's Faith

For The Love of Christian Homemaking

The Prentiss Study (Free Download)

Early Morning Revival Challenge

[Cover photo: Part of the Grounds at Mrs. White's Vermont Estate]

Early Morning Revival Challenge

With Journaling,
Prayer,
Reading Psalms and Proverbs,
And Quotes from Ministers.

-90 – Day Bible Study –

The Legacy of Home Press
puritanlight@gmail.com

The Legacy of Home Press
ISBN-13: 978-0615861050
ISBN-10: 0615861059
Early Morning Revival Challenge
Author – Mrs. Sharon White

Contents

Early Morning Revival Challenge

Early Morning Revival Challenge

Preface

John Wesley, in the 1700's, began the habit of writing down an account of how he spent his time. He was motivated by advice given by Bishop Taylor, in his book, "*Rules for Holy Living and Dying*." He began adding reflections, and including the work he was doing for Christ. I was amazed to see, in his routine, that he scheduled prayer for 3 hours each day, despite how busy he was! His custom was to rise at 4 a.m. and pray until 5 a.m. He had midday public prayers, and then evening prayers, alone, for an hour. I am inspired and *convicted!*

The publisher of Wesley's complete works, in 1831 said:

"Mr. Wesley's life was one of the greatest activity. He published more books, travelled more miles, and preached more sermons, than any other Minister of his age; and the entire history of human nature does not furnish a higher example of laborious diligence in the service of God and man."

A few years ago, I was able to obtain a set of his writings. There are thousands of pages. The set includes his journals, his sermons, and his letters. It is an astounding resource.

It used to be a common practice for people to keep a journal of their time, which produced a history of their life. In this modern day, we are so "busy" living, that we take little time to reflect and to record.

Our prayers are rushed and often by rote. Our Bible reading (as a general rule) is seriously lacking; often commenced with feeble efforts. The greatest help I have found, to keep me on a godly path, is to read the words from great ministers of long ago. These are the dedicated men who preached, and wrote, and took care of the great masses of people in their day. These men were writing and praying and studying in a time before modern transportation made it fast and easy to travel. It was a time before "wholesome" entertainment was brought into our homes by way of television and computer. These men were not distracted by our modern amusements.

I have, in my home library, a collection of sermons and writings from ministers. My own Grandfather and Uncle were revival preachers. My father's library contains many works of dedicated ministers. Over time, I have added select volumes of the writings of Charles Spurgeon, Richard Baxter, Thomas Watson, and many more. Two of my most treasured books were published 200 years ago. These little volumes were found in an antique bookstore in London and shipped to me as a gift from a British friend. The books are the writings of John Bunyan, and Thomas Boston. The text in one of the books is difficult to read. It was from a time when printers used a typeface that made our modern "s" look like an "f." The pages are also well - worn and aged. The books, and the writings, are ancient but are highly valuable.

The Revival Challenge

- I have selected 90 quotes from the words of the various ministers for a 90 day challenge.

- I ask that you write in a journal each day, like Wesley.

- I ask you to pray, and to read passages from the Bible.

- These short assignments are designed to be done early in the morning.

- I ask you to rise 30 - 60 minutes before you normally would.

- I ask you to spend 20 minutes doing the daily challenge, each day, for 90 days.

Then let us just see what revival will take place in your heart, soul, and mind!

Directions

I have set up a checklist for each of the 90 days. All you have to do is complete each assignment, and place a checkmark beside it.

Make a commitment to get up earlier than normal, each morning, to do the program. Just like an athlete, training for a marathon, would make the sacrifice and extra effort, we will be getting up earlier and doing this challenge.

You will need a Bible. We will be reading through the entire books of Psalms and Proverbs. There are specific daily passages to read, in order, so that both books are completed by the end of the study.

Spend some time in prayer. This could be time of praise, of praying about concerns, family members, friends or whatever is laid on your heart.

A quote from a Minister is listed on each day. Please read each day's quote and think about it for at least a few minutes.

You will need a notebook. This is where you will be writing your daily journal entries. Please put a date and time on each one. Some suggestions of what to write: Your thoughts from the day's assignments; what is going on in your life; blessings; worries that you are taking to God; or anything you would be blessed by looking back, and reading over, at the end of the 90 days.

Please do not miss a single day. This program is a **discipline**. It is a challenge. Please take the time to complete each day's work.

Get ready for a revival!

The Study

Day 1

Date _____ Time _____
Read Psalms chapters 1 and 2 _____
Pray _____
Read today's Quote _____

"I believe God spake to many hearts; but who will obey his voice?"
- John Wesley, 1769

Write in your journal _____

Day 2

Date _____ Time _____
Read Psalms chapters 3 and 4 _____
Pray _____
Read today's Quote _____

"I stood in the main street, and cried to a numerous congregation,
'Fear God, and keep his commandments; for this is the whole of
man.'" - John Wesley, 1769

Write in your journal _____

Day 3

Date _____ Time _____
Read Psalms chapters 5 and 6 _____
Pray _____
Read today's Quote _____

"Both here and at Pembroke, I found the people in general to be in a cold, dead, languid state.   And no wonder, since there had been for several months a total neglect of discipline. I did all I could to awaken them once more, and then left them full of good resolutions." - John Wesley, 1774

Write in your journal _____

Day 4

Date _____ Time _____
Read Psalms chapters 7 and 8 _____
Pray _____
Read today's Quote _____

" 'The child of many prayers,' said an old Christian to Augustine's mother, 'shall never perish.' " - J. C. Ryle, 1800's

Write in your journal _____

Day 5

Date _____ Time _____
Read Psalms chapters 9 and 10 _____
Pray _____
Read today's Quote _____

"Have you forgotten the lives that many live? Can we really believe that people are praying against sin night and day, when we see them plunging into it? Can we suppose they pray against the world, when they are entirely absorbed and taken up with its pursuits? Can we think they really ask God for grace to serve him, when they do not show the slightest desire to serve him at all?" - J. C. Ryle, 1800's

Write in your journal _____

Day 6

Date _____ Time _____
Read Psalms chapters 11 and 12 _____
Pray _____
Read today's Quote _____

"Diligence in prayer is the secret of eminent holiness." - J. C. Ryle, 1800's

Write in your journal _____

Day 7

Date _____ Time _____
Read Psalms chapters 13 and 14 _____
Pray _____
Read today's Quote _____

"Prayer can lighten crosses for us, however heavy. It can bring down to our side One who will help us to bear them. Prayer can open a door for us when our way seems hedged up. It can bring down One who will say, 'This is the way, walk in it.' Prayer can let in a ray of hope when all our earthly prospects seem darkened."
- J. C. Ryle, 1800's

Write in your journal _____

Day 8

Date _____ Time _____
Read Psalms chapters 15 and 16 _____
Pray _____
Read today's Quote _____

"I am sure that this is the best fruit of the cross, when we, from the hard fare of the dear inn, cry the more that God would send a fair wind, to land us, hungered and oppressed strangers, at the door of our Father's house, which now is made, in Christ, our kindly heritage."
- Samuel Rutherford, 1637

Write in your journal _____

Day 9

Date _____ Time _____
Read Psalms chapters 17 and 18 _____
Pray _____
Read today's Quote _____

[Describing Samuel Rutherford, known as "one of the most moving and affectionate preachers in his time, or perhaps in any age of the church."]

"See him passing along yonder field, and climbing that hill on his way to some cottage, his 'face upward' for the most part, as if he were gazing into heaven. He has time to visit, for he rises at three in the morning, and at that early hour meets his God in prayer and meditation, and has space for study besides." - Rev. Andrew A Bonar.

Write in your journal _____

Day 10

Date _____ Time _____
Read Psalms chapters 19 and 20 _____
Pray _____
Read today's Quote _____

"The Lord hath told you what you should be doing till He come. 'Wait and hasten,' saith Peter, 'for the coming of the Lord.' Sigh and long for the dawning of that morning, and the breaking of that day, of the coming of the Son of Man, when the shadows shall flee away. Wait with the wearied night-watch for the breaking of the eastern sky."
- Samuel Rutherford, 1600's

Write in your journal _____

Day 11

Date _____ Time _____

Read Psalms chapters 21 and 22 _____
Pray _____
Read today's Quote _____

"I urge upon you. . . a nearer communion with Christ, and a growing communion. There are curtains to be drawn by in Christ, that we never saw, and new folding of love in Him. . . Therefore, dig deep; and sweat, and labour, and take pains for Him; and set by as much time in the day for Him as you can." - Samuel Rutherford, 1600's

Write in your journal _____

Day 12

Date _____ Time _____
Read Psalms chapters 23 and 24 _____
Pray _____
Read today's Quote _____

"Let not the world be your portion. . . set your heart on the inheritance. Go up beforehand, and see your lodging. Look through all your Father's rooms in heaven: In your Father's house are many dwelling - places. Men take a sight of lands ere they buy them. I know that Christ hath made the bargain already; but be kind to the house you are going to, and see it often. Set your heart on things that are above, where Christ is at the right hand of God."
 - Samuel Rutherford, 1600's

Write in your journal _____

Day 13

Date _____ Time _____

Read Psalms chapters 25 and 26 _____
Pray _____
Read today's Quote _____

"There is no way of quieting the mind, and of silencing the heart of a mother, but godly submission." - Samuel Rutherford, 1600's

Write in your journal _____

Day 14

Date _____ Time _____
Read Psalms chapters 27 and 28 _____
Pray _____
Read today's Quote _____

"And blessed shall he be who shall blow the trumpet to cause other sleeping ones awake, and shall help to build the wastes, and the fallen tabernacle of David." - Samuel Rutherford, 1600's

Write in your journal _____

Day 15

Date _____ Time _____

Read Psalms chapters 29 and 30 _____
Pray _____
Read today's Quote _____

"I have wrestled on towards Heaven,
 'Gainst storm, and wind, and tide : --
Now, like a weary traveller,
That leaneth on his guide,
Amid the shades of evening,
While sinks life's ling'ring sand,
I hail the glory dawning
From Immanuel's land."

- Samuel Rutherford, 1600's

Write in your journal _____

Day 16

Date _____ Time _____
Read Psalms chapters 31 and 32 _____
Pray _____
Read today's Quote _____

"The still and quiet soul is like a ship that lies still and quiet in the
harbour; you may take in what goods, what commodities you
please, whilst the ship lies quiet and still: so when the soul is quiet
and still under the hand of God, it is most fitted, and advantaged to
take in much of God, of Christ, of heaven." - Thomas Brooks, 1811

Write in your journal _____

Day 17

Date _____ Time _____

Read Psalms chapters 33 and 34 _____
Pray _____
Read today's Quote _____

"A soul truly noble will sooner part with all, than the peace of a good conscience." - Thomas Brooks, 1811

Write in your journal _____

Day 18

Date _____ Time _____
Read Psalms chapters 35 and 36 _____
Pray _____
Read today's Quote _____

"It will be our sin and shame, if we do not bear up with patience and silence under all our sufferings, considering what an admirable copy Christ hath set before us." - Thomas Brooks, 1811

Write in your journal _____

Day 19

Date _____ Time _____

Read Psalms chapters 37 and 38 _____
Pray _____
Read today's Quote _____

"The more thy afflictions are increased, the more thy heart shall be raised heaven-wards." - Thomas Brooks, 1811

Write in your journal _____

Day 20

Date _____ Time _____
Read Psalms chapters 39 and 40 _____
Pray _____
Read today's Quote _____

"Luther could not understand some psalms, till he was afflicted." - Thomas Brooks, 1811

Write in your journal _____

Day 21

Date _____ Time _____

Read Psalms chapters 41 and 42 _____
Pray _____
Read today's Quote _____

"Many read good books, and yet get nothing, because they read them over cursorily, slightly, superficially: but he that would read to profit, must then, Read, and look up for a blessing." - Thomas Brooks, 1811

Write in your journal _____

Day 22

Date _____ Time _____
Read Psalms chapters 43 and 44 _____
Pray _____
Read today's Quote _____

"He that would read to profit, must read and meditate. Meditation is the food of your souls." Thomas Brooks, 1811

Write in your journal _____

Day 23

Date _____ Time _____

Read Psalms chapters 45 and 46 _____
Pray _____
Read today's Quote _____

"Prayer (saith Augustine) without meditation is dry and formal; and reading without meditation is useless and unprofitable."
 - Thomas Brooks, 1811

Write in your journal _____

Day 24

Date _____ Time _____
Read Psalms chapters 47 and 48 _____
Pray _____
Read today's Quote _____

"Surely by these trials and troubles the Lord will fix my soul more than ever upon the great concernments of another world."
 - Thomas Boston, 1811

Write in your journal _____

Day 25

Date _____ Time _____

Read Psalms chapters 49 and 50 _____
Pray _____
Read today's Quote _____

"Though Calvin, under his greatest pains, was never heard to mutter, nor murmur, yet he was heard often to say, *'How long, Lord, how long?'* " - Thomas Boston, 1811

Write in your journal _____

Day 26

Date _____ Time _____
Read Psalms chapters 51 and 52 _____
Pray _____
Read today's Quote _____

"There is no water so sweet as the saints tears."
- Thomas Boston, 1811

Write in your journal _____

Day 27

Date _____ Time _____

Read Psalms chapters 53 and 54 _____
Pray _____
Read today's Quote _____

"We must always converse with God in our minds and thoughts."
- Samuel Annesley, 1661

Write in your journal _____

Day 28

Date _____ Time _____
Read Psalms chapters 55 and 56 _____
Pray _____
Read today's Quote _____

"When you eat and drink to the glory of God, sleep no more than
may make you serviceable unto God; when your solitary musings are
about the engaging of your souls to God; when your social
conference is about the things of God; when all acts of worship
endear God to you; when all your duties bring you nearer to God;
when the love of God is the sweetness of your mercies, and your
cordial under afflictions; when you can love God under amazing
providences, as well as under refreshing deliverances; then you may
be said to love God with all your souls." - Samuel Annesley, 1661

Write in your journal _____

Day 29

Date _____ Time _____

Read Psalms chapters 57 and 58 _____
Pray _____
Read today's Quote _____

"Be suspicious of every thing that may steal away or divert your love from God." - Samuel Annesley, 1661

Write in your journal _____

Day 30

Date _____ Time _____
Read Psalms chapters 59 and 60 _____
Pray _____
Read today's Quote _____

"Every thing of religion is at first uncouth; the work of mortification is harsh, and the work of holiness difficult; but practice will facilitate them, and make thee in love with them; so the more thou aquaintest thyself with God, the more thou [wilt] love him." - Samuel Annesley, 1661

Write in your journal _____

Day 31

Date _____ Time _____

Read Psalms chapters 61 and 62 _____
Pray _____
Read today's Quote _____

"Observation shows that families which have no household worship, are at a low ebb in spiritual things; that families where it is performed in a cold, sluggish, negligent, or hurried way, are little affected by it, and little affected by any means of grace; and that families where God is worshipped, every morning and evening, by all the inmates of the house in a solemn and affectionate service, are blessed with increase of piety and happiness. Every individual is blessed. Each one receives a portion of the heavenly food." - James W. Alexander, 1847

Write in your journal _____

Day 32

Date _____ Time _____
Read Psalms chapters 63 and 64 _____
Pray _____
Read today's Quote _____

"Better a roofless, than a prayerless house."
- James W. Alexander, 1847

Write in your journal _____

Day 33

Date _____ Time _____

Read Psalms chapters 65 and 66 _____
Pray _____
Read today's Quote _____

"In Greenland, when a stranger knocks at a door, he asks, 'Is God in this house?' and if they answer, 'Yes,' he enters."
 - James W. Alexander, 1847

Write in your journal _____

Day 34

Date _____ Time _____
Read Psalms chapters 67 and 68 _____
Pray _____
Read today's Quote _____

"The daily regular and solemn reading of God's holy word, by a parent before his children, is one of the most powerful agencies of a Christian life." - James W. Alexander, 1847

Write in your journal _____

Day 35

Date _____ Time _____

Read Psalms chapters 69 and 70 _____
Pray _____
Read today's Quote _____

"In families where there is daily praise of God, in psalms and hymns and spiritual songs, there is an additional influence on the young."
 - James W. Alexander, 1847

Write in your journal _____

Day 36

Date _____ Time _____
Read Psalms chapters 71 and 72 _____
Pray _____
Read today's Quote _____

"To reside, even as a servant, in a family where the worship of God is duly observed, is an unspeakable privilege."
 - James W. Alexander, 1847

Write in your journal _____

Day 37

Date _____ Time _____

Read Psalms chapters 73 and 74 _____
Pray _____
Read today's Quote _____

"Family worship includes the reading of the Scriptures; and this in itself is one of the most valuable instruments of cultivating the powers. It is a world of knowledge in itself. The truths which it presents are the greatest and the most awakening which can be subjected to human attention. It is the voice of God." - James W. Alexander, 1847

Write in your journal _____

Day 38

Date _____ Time _____
Read Psalms chapters 75 and 76 _____
Pray _____
Read today's Quote _____

"In a word, we cannot think it possible for any family to enjoy, twice every day for all their lives, the privilege of hearing the Scriptures read at domestic worship, without, by that very means, rising perceptibly and greatly in knowledge and intellectual force."
- James W. Alexander, 1847

Write in your journal _____

Day 39

Date _____ Time _____

Read Psalms chapters 77 and 78 _____
Pray _____
Read today's Quote _____

"Let it not be thought, because the Bible is simply heard, by the majority of a household, that it falls without effect. Hearing is study, and of the most ancient kind. Before copies of the word of God were multiplied, as in our happy day, it was by the ear, and not by the eye,
that its contents were mostly received. When the manner of reading is good, it is still the most impressive method, for the ignorant and the young. By such means, the Family- Worship becomes a household school, and the tuition goes on for a lifetime."
- James W. Alexander, 1847

Write in your journal _____

Day 40

Date _____ Time _____
Read Psalms chapters 79 and 80 _____
Pray _____
Read today's Quote _____

"Texts and principles poured into the most careless, or we might even say, the most unwilling mind, and prayers uttered even before the undevout, will now and then recur, as suggestions, and be owned with saving effect." - James W. Alexander, 1847

Write in your journal _____

Day 41

Date _____ Time _____

Read Psalms chapters 81 and 82 _____
Pray _____
Read today's Quote _____

"Never did a man look upon Christ with a spiritual eye, but he went away quite changed." - Thomas Watson, 1653

Write in your journal _____

Day 42

Date _____ Time _____
Read Psalms chapters 83 and 84 _____
Pray _____
Read today's Quote _____

"A ship that lies at anchor may sometimes be a little shaken, but never sinks: flesh and blood may have its fears and disquiets, but grace doth check them. A Christian having cast anchor in heaven, his heart never sinks; a gracious spirit is a contented spirit." - Thomas Watson, 1653

Write in your journal _____

Day 43

Date _____ Time _____

Read Psalms chapters 85 and 86 _____
Pray _____
Read today's Quote _____

"Outward troubles cannot hinder this blessed contentment; it is a spiritual thing, and ariseth from spiritual grounds, namely, the apprehension of God's love." - Thomas Watson, 1653

Write in your journal _____

Day 44

Date _____ Time _____
Read Psalms chapters 87 and 88 _____
Pray _____
Read today's Quote _____

"If your estate be small, yet God can bless a little. It is not how much money we have, but how much blessing." - Thomas Watson, 1653

Write in your journal _____

Day 45

Date _____ Time _____

Read Psalms chapters 89 and 90 _____
Pray _____
Read today's Quote _____

"Where there is too much worldly care, there is too little spiritual [duty]." - Thomas Watson, 1653

Write in your journal _____

Day 46

Date _____ Time _____
Read Psalms chapters 91 and 92 _____
Pray _____
Read today's Quote _____

"Faith carries up the soul, and makes it aspire after more noble and generous delights than earth affords." - Thomas Watson, 1653

Write in your journal _____

Day 47

Date _____ Time _____

Read Psalms chapters 93 and 94 _____
Pray _____
Read today's Quote _____

"Methinks the smoothness of the end should make amends for the ruggedness of the way. O eternity, eternity! Think often of the kingdom prepared." - Thomas Watson, 1653

Write in your journal _____

Day 48

Date _____ Time _____
Read Psalms chapters 95 and 96 _____
Pray _____
Read today's Quote _____

"Art thou contented, O christian, with a little? Thou shalt see greater things than these: God will distill the sweet influences of his love into thy soul; he will raise thee up friends; he will bless the oil in the cruse; and when that is done, he will crown thee with an eternal enjoyment of himself; he will give thee heaven, where thou shalt have as much
contentment as thy soul can possibly thirst after."
- Thomas Watson, 1653

Write in your journal _____

Day 49

Date _____ Time _____

Read Psalms chapters 97 and 98 _____
Pray _____
Read today's Quote _____

"True repentance is a turning to God, and setting of our hearts and hope on heaven; so that we now love holiness, and seek God's kingdom above this world." - Richard Baxter, 1600's

Write in your journal _____

Day 50

Date _____ Time _____
Read Psalms chapters 99 and 100 _____
Pray _____
Read today's Quote _____

"It is pity, saith Mr. Bolton, that christians should ever meet together without some talk of their meeting in heaven, or the way to it, before they part." - Richard Baxter, 1600's

Write in your journal _____

Day 51

Date _____ Time _____

Read Psalms chapters 101 and 102 _____
Pray _____
Read today's Quote _____

"Art thou delighting thyself in the society of the saints?"
- Richard Baxter, 1600's

Write in your journal _____

Day 52

Date _____ Time _____
Read Psalms chapters 103 and 104 _____
Pray _____
Read today's Quote _____

"As man in innocency did know that he was not his own, so he knew that nothing that he had was his own; but that he was the steward of his Creator, for whom he was to use them, and to whom he was accountable." - Richard Baxter, 1600's

Write in your journal _____

Day 53

Date _____ Time _____

Read Psalms chapters 105 and 106 _____
Pray _____
Read today's Quote _____

"Walk before the Lord: live, and think, and speak as in his presence." - Richard Baxter, 1600's

Write in your journal _____

Day 54

Date _____ Time _____
Read Psalms chapters 107 and 108 _____
Pray _____
Read today's Quote _____

"If persons are seen firm in principle; fearless in duty; zealous in the cause of God; yet humble and lowly; and gentle and tender; and patient in suffering; and ready to forgive -- no one need to be told with whom *they* have been." - William Jay, 1800's

Write in your journal _____

Day 55

Date _____ Time _____

Read Psalms chapters 109 and 110 _____
Pray _____
Read today's Quote _____

"Tell me a man's company, and I will tell you his character. . . All association, however limited, produces some influence."
- William Jay, 1800's

Write in your journal _____

Day 56

Date _____ Time _____
Read Psalms chapters 111 and 112 _____
Pray _____
Read today's Quote _____

"So if you are proud, and vain, and worldly-minded, and avaricious, and revengeful, and censurious, and unkind, we do not require you to tell us with whom you are most intimate." - William Jay, 1800's

Write in your journal _____

Day 57

Date _____ Time _____

Read Psalms chapters 113 and 114 _____
Pray _____
Read today's Quote _____

"But, Oh! My Father's house!
 Here, toil; there, rest.
Here, trouble; there, joy and gladness.
 Here, darkness; there, light.
Here, sin; there, spotless purity."
- William Jay, 1800's

Write in your journal _____

Day 58

Date _____ Time _____
Read Psalms chapters 115 and 116 _____
Pray _____
Read today's Quote _____

"The grand rule of obedience, is the will of God. And the language
of the Christian is, Lord, what wilt thou have me to do?"
 - William Jay, 1800's

Write in your journal _____

Day 59

Date _____ Time _____

Read Psalms chapters 117 and 118 _____
Pray _____
Read today's Quote _____

"Persons and families are, especially among the common people, always unkind, and rude, and savage, both in their temper and manners, where the Sabbath is neglected. But they are respectful, and humane, and tender, where it is observed; because they see each other to advantage, and mingle under moral and religious impressions, which, though not always powerful enough to sanctify, contribute to soften and civilize." - William Jay, 1800's

Write in your journal _____

Day 60

Date _____ Time _____
Read Psalms chapters 119 and 120 _____
Pray _____
Read today's Quote _____

"He that is slothful doth his work by halves; and so it is with him that is slothful for heaven." - John Bunyan, 1600's

Write in your journal _____

Day 61

Date _____ Time _____

Read Psalms chapters 121 and 122 _____
Pray _____
Read today's Quote _____

"What shall I say? Time runs; and will you still be slothful?"
  - John Bunyan, 1600's

Write in your journal _____

Day 62

Date _____ Time _____
Read Psalms chapters 123 and 124 _____
Pray _____
Read today's Quote _____

"Arise, man! Be slothful no longer: set heart and foot, and all the
way to God, and run; the crown is at the end of the race; there also
standeth the heavenly Forerunner, even Jesus, who hath prepared
heavenly provision to make thy soul welcome."
  - John Bunyan, 1600's

Write in your journal _____

Day 63

Date _____ Time _____

Read Psalms chapters 125 and 126 _____
Pray _____
Read today's Quote _____

"Set to work, and when thou hast run thyself down weary, then the Lord Jesus will take thee up and carry thee."   - John Bunyan, 1600's

Write in your journal _____

Day 64

Date _____ Time _____
Read Psalms chapters 127 and 128 _____
Pray _____
Read today's Quote _____

"I beseech you, in the name of our Lord Jesus Christ, that none of you do run so lazily in the road to heaven as to hinder either yourselves or others." - John Bunyan, 1600's

Write in your journal _____

Day 65

Date _____ Time _____

Read Psalms chapters 129 and 130 _____
Pray _____
Read today's Quote _____

"A taste of the transcendent goodness of God, the hidden excellency of religion, would hold you fast to the right side."
- Thomas Boston, 1700's

Write in your journal _____

Day 66

Date _____ Time _____
Read Psalms chapters 131 and 132 _____
Pray _____
Read today's Quote _____

"They would fain be at heaven, but have no heart for the rugged way to it. . . The sluggard loves the gold, but will not dig for it."
- Thomas Boston, 1700's

Write in your journal _____

Day 67

Date _____ Time _____

Read Psalms chapters 133 and 134 _____
Pray _____
Read today's Quote _____

"Put on a resolution, a peremptory resolution for God, to cleave to
him at any rate, and to pass through the wilderness to the heavenly
Canaan, cost what it will."
- Thomas Boston, 1700's

Write in your journal _____

Day 68

Date _____ Time _____
Read Psalms chapters 135 and 136 _____
Pray _____
Read today's Quote _____

"Beware of wavering, and study to be stable Christians. . . Stability
is the beginning of comfortable experiences in religion. We cannot
think to thrive in a trade, till we settle to it. A fool is always
beginning, leaves off, begins again, and so on; he never brings
anything to perfection." - Thomas Boston, 1700's

Write in your journal _____

Day 69

Date _____ Time _____

Read Psalms chapters 137 and 138 _____
Pray _____
Read today's Quote _____

"There is the mixed band of the world's cares. These are the world's
thorn-hedge, which the Christian must break through, or else they
will choke the seed of the word in his heart. This is the thorny
crown it sets upon our heads so soon as we set out into the world.
How hard it is to keep our ground here!" - Thomas Boston, 1700's

Write in your journal _____

Day 70

Date _____ Time _____
Read Psalms chapters 139 and 140 _____
Pray _____
Read today's Quote _____

"The world lieth in wickedness; it is hard to bear out, against the
stream of example set before us. To be righteous as Noah in his
generation, to keep clean garments in Sardis, is not easy." - Thomas
Boston, 1700's

Write in your journal _____

Day 71

Date _____ Time _____

Read Psalms chapters 141 and 142 _____
Pray _____
Read today's Quote _____

"Draw near as servants of the house, to serve our Lord, to wait upon him, and behold his glory." - Thomas Boston, 1700's

Write in your journal _____

Day 72

Date _____ Time _____
Read Psalms chapters 143 and 144 _____
Pray _____
Read today's Quote _____

"I told you last Sabbath, that you may draw near to God in Christ, and that you ought to draw near. Is there any here who so love their outcast condition, that they will not come back, nor draw near to God, though they are invited." - Thomas Boston, 1700's

Write in your journal _____

Day 73

Date _____ Time _____

Read Psalms chapters 145 and 146 _____
Pray _____
Read today's Quote _____

"You must learn to say, *Thy will be done*. Put away your self-will.
The will of his commandments must determine your practice; the
will of his providence, your lot. The long quarrel betwixt the Lord
and you must now be at an end, namely, whether your will or his
shall be done." - Thomas Boston, 1700's

Write in your journal _____

Day 74

Date _____ Time _____
Read Psalms chapters 147 and 148 _____
Pray _____
Read today's Quote _____

"We have been guilty of murmuring at his will; but yet our newborn
nature evermore at its core and center knoweth that the will of the
Lord is wise and good; and we therefore bow our heads with
reverent agreement, and say, 'Not as I will, but as thou wilt.' "
- Charles Haddon Spurgeon, 1800's

Write in your journal _____

Day 75

Date _____ Time _____

Read Psalms chapters 149 and 150 _____

Pray _____

Read today's Quote _____

"O that we might cease to be with our God as wayfaring men who tarry but for a night: may we *dwell* in God, and may he dwell in us. Walking implies *action;* and our actions should always be in the Lord." - Charles Haddon Spurgeon, 1800's

Write in your journal _____

Day 76

Date _____ Time _____

Read Proverbs chapters 1 and 2 _____

Pray _____

Read today's Quote _____

"We may be confirmed in our anxious desire to have the Lord walking with us in this thing, when we consider the blessings which are sure to flow from his presence. Ah! What holy quickening shall come upon every one of us." - Charles Haddon Spurgeon, 1800's

Write in your journal _____

Day 77

Date _____ Time _____

Read Proverbs chapters 3 and 4 _____
Pray _____
Read today's Quote _____

"If I love the world, the love of the Father is not in me; consequently he cannot walk with me, for we are not agreed."
 - Charles Haddon Spurgeon, 1800's

Write in your journal _____

Day 78

Date _____ Time _____
Read Proverbs chapters 5 and 6 _____
Pray _____
Read today's Quote _____

"This is a noisy age, and the Church of Christ herself is too noisy. We have very little silent worship, I fear. I do not so much regret the absence of silence from the public assembly as from our private devotions, where it has a sacred hallowing - influence, unspeakably valuable." - Charles Haddon Spurgeon, 1800's

Write in your journal _____

Day 79

Date _____ Time _____

Read Proverbs chapters 7 and 8 _____
Pray _____
Read today's Quote _____

"Keep silence, then, ye saints, till ye have felt your folly and your
weakness, and then renew your strength most gloriously by casting
yourselves upon the strength of God."
- Charles Haddon Spurgeon, 1800's

Write in your journal _____

Day 80

Date _____ Time _____
Read Proverbs chapters 9 and 10 _____
Pray _____
Read today's Quote _____

"All the mighty works of God, have been attended with great prayer,
as well as with great faith." - Charles Haddon Spurgeon, 1800's

Write in your journal _____

Day 81

Date _____ Time _____

Read Proverbs chapters 11 and 12 _____
Pray _____
Read today's Quote _____

"Religion is not a sometime thing, only secondary in importance, or the thing "by the by," proper only for spare hours; but it must be the grand business of our lives." - Thomas Watson, 1600's

Write in your journal _____

Day 82

Date _____ Time _____
Read Proverbs chapters 13 and 14 _____
Pray _____
Read today's Quote _____

"This is to make religion our business, when we are so taken up with it that we have scarcely any leisure for other things. Christian, you have a God to serve and a soul to save; and if you have anything of religion in you, you will take heed of the thieves of time, and will reserve all opportunities for the best things. How far are they from Christianity who jostle out holy duties! Instead of borrowing time from the world for prayer, they steal time from prayer that they might follow the world." - Thomas Watson, 1600's

Write in your journal _____

Day 83

Date _____ Time _____

Read Proverbs chapters 15 and 16 _____
Pray _____
Read today's Quote _____

"The godly, entering upon their celestial reward, are said to enter into the joy of their Lord, Matthew 25:21. Oh, amazing! The saints enter into God's own joy. They have not only the joy which God bestows, but the joy which God enjoys." - Thomas Watson, 1600's

Write in your journal _____

Day 84

Date _____ Time _____
Read Proverbs chapters 17 and 18 _____
Pray _____
Read today's Quote _____

"Think what God has prepared for those who love Him! Oh, that our thoughts would ascend! The higher the bird flies the sweeter it sings." - Thomas Watson, 1600's

Write in your journal _____

Day 85

Date _____ Time _____

Read Proverbs chapters 19 and 20 _____
Pray _____
Read today's Quote _____

"When we grow careless of keeping our souls, then God recovers our taste of good things again by sharp crosses." - Richard Sibbes, 1600's

Write in your journal _____

Day 86

Date _____ Time _____
Read Proverbs chapters 21 and 22 _____
Pray _____
Read today's Quote _____

"He that now loves God, that delights and rejoices in him with an humble joy, and holy delight, and an obedient love, is a child of God." - John Wesley, 1700's

Write in your journal _____

Day 87

Date _____ Time _____

Read Proverbs chapters 23 and 24 _____
Pray _____
Read today's Quote _____

"Our immediate fruit of patience is peace: A sweet tranquility of
mind; a serenity of spirit, which can never be found, unless where
patience reigns. And this peace often rises into joy. Even in the
midst of various temptations, those that are enabled 'in patience to
possess their souls,' can witness, not only quietness of spirit, but
triumph and exultation." - John Wesley, 1700's

Write in your journal _____

Day 88

Date _____ Time _____
Read Proverbs chapters 25 and 26 _____
Pray _____
Read today's Quote _____

"Awake, thou everlasting spirit, out of thy dream of worldly
happiness! Did not God create thee for himself? Then thou canst
not rest till thou restest in him. Return, thou wanderer! Fly back to
the ark. This is not thy home." - Charles Wesley, 1742

Write in your journal _____

Day 89

Date _____ Time _____

Read Proverbs chapters 27 and 28 _____
Pray _____
Read today's Quote _____

"O may the Angel of the Lord come upon thee, and the light shine into thy prison! And mayest thou feel the stroke of an Almighty Hand, raising thee, with, 'Arise up quickly, gird thyself, and bind on thy sandals, cast thy garments about thee, and follow me.' "
- Charles Wesley, 1742

Write in your journal _____

Day 90

Date _____ Time _____
Read Proverbs chapters 29, 30 and 31 _____
Pray _____
Read today's Quote _____

"Turn us again, O Lord God of Hosts! Show the light of thy countenance, and we shall be whole." - Charles Wesley, 1742

Write in your journal _____

End of Study -

Bibliography of Quotes

Day 1 (Page 15)

Page 354, "*The Works of John Wesley*" volume 3, published by Baker Books.

Day 2 (Page 15)

Page 363, "*The Works of John Wesley*" volume 3, published by Baker Books.

Day 3 (Page 16)

Page 26, "*The Works of John Wesley*" volume 4, published by Baker Books.

Day 4 (Page 16)

Page 17, "*A Call to Prayer,*" published by Audubon Press.

Day 5 (Page 17)

Page 15, "*A Call to Prayer,*" published by Audubon Press.

Day 6 (Page 17)

Page 18, "*A Call to Prayer,*" published by Audubon Press.

Day 7 (Page 18)

Page 24, "*A Call to Prayer,*" published by Audubon Press.

Day 8 (Page 18)

Page 178, "*Letters of Samuel Rutherford*" Published by Still Waters Revival Books.

Day 9 (Page 19)

Page 5, "*Letters of Samuel Rutherford*" Published by Still Waters Revival Books.

Day 10 (Page 19)

Page 30, "*Letters of Samuel Rutherford*" Published by Still Waters Revival Books.

Day 11 (Page 20)

Page 214, "*Letters of Samuel Rutherford*" Published by Still Waters Revival Books.

Day 12 (Page 20)

Page 214, "*Letters of Samuel Rutherford*" Published by Still Waters Revival Books.

Day 13 (Page 21)

Page 700, "*Letters of Samuel Rutherford*" Published by Still Waters Revival Books.

Day 14 (Page 21)

Page 708, "*Letters of Samuel Rutherford*" Published by Still Waters Revival Books.

Day 15 (Page 22)

Page 743, "*Letters of Samuel Rutherford*" Published by Still Waters Revival Books.

Day 16 (Page 22)

Page 70, "*The Mute Christian under the Smarting Rod*," Published by Still Waters Revival Books.

Day 17 (Page 23)

Page 89, "*The Mute Christian under the Smarting Rod*," Published by Still Waters Revival Books.

Day 18 (Page 23)

Page 67, "*The Mute Christian under the Smarting Rod*," Published by Still Waters Revival Books.

Day 19 (Page 24)

Preface, "*The Mute Christian under the Smarting Rod*," Published by Still Waters Revival Books.

Day 20 (Page 24)

Preface, "*The Mute Christian under the Smarting Rod*," Published by Still Waters Revival Books.

Day 21 (Page 25)

Preface, "The *Mute Christian under the Smarting Rod*," Published by Still Waters Revival Books.

Day 22 (Page 25)

Preface, "*The Mute Christian under the Smarting Rod,*" Published by Still Waters Revival Books.

Day 23 (Page 26)

Preface, "*The Mute Christian under the Smarting Rod*," Published by Still Waters Revival Books.

Day 24 (Page 26)

Page 39, "*The Mute Christian under the Smarting Rod*," Published by Still Waters Revival Books.

Day 25 (Page 27)

Page 48, "*The Mute Christian under the Smarting Rod*," Published by Still Waters Revival Books.

Day 26 (Page 27)

Page 55, "*The Mute Christian under the Smarting Rod*," Published by Still Waters Revival Books.

Day 27 (Page 28)

Page 579, "*How We May Attain to Love God with all our Hearts, Souls, and Minds,*" published by Still Waters Revival Books.

Day 28 (Page 28)

Page 578, "*How We May Attain to Love God with all our Hearts, Souls, and Minds*," published by Still Waters Revival Books.

Day 29 (Page 29)

Page 586, "*How We May Attain to Love God with all our Hearts, Souls, and Minds*," published by Still Waters Revival Books.

Day 30 (Page 29)

Page 598, "*How We May Attain to Love God with all our Hearts, Souls, and Minds*," published by Still Waters Revival Books.

Day 31 (Page 30)

Page 35, "*Family Worship: Its Influence Over All of Life*," published by Still Waters Revival Books.

Day 32 (Page 30)

Page 57, "*Family Worship: Its Influence Over All of Life*," published by Still Waters Revival Books.

Day 33 (Page 31)

Page 59, "*Family Worship: Its Influence Over All of Life*," published by Still Waters Revival Books.

Day 34 (Page 31)

Page 62, "*Family Worship: Its Influence Over All of Life*," published by Still Waters Revival Books.

Day 35 (Page 32)

Page 65, "*Family Worship: Its Influence Over All of Life*," published by Still Waters Revival Books.

Day 36 (Page 32)

Page 74, "*Family Worship: Its Influence Over All of Life*," published by Still Waters Revival Books.

Day 37 (Page 33)

Page 84, "*Family Worship: Its Influence Over All of Life*," published by Still Waters Revival Books.

Day 38 (Page 33)

Page 87, "*Family Worship: Its Influence Over All of Life*," published by Still Waters Revival Books.

Day 39 (Page 34)

Page 87, "*Family Worship: Its Influence Over All of Life*," published by Still Waters Revival Books.

Day 40 (Page 34)

Page 91, "*Family Worship: Its Influence Over All of Life*," published by Still Waters Revival Books.

Day 41 (Page 35)

Page 10, "*The Art of Divine Contentment*" published by Still Waters Revival Books.

Day 42 (Page 35)

Page 26, "*The Art of Divine Contentment*" published by Still Waters Revival Books.

Day 43 (Page 36)

Page 33, "*The Art of Divine Contentment*" published by Still Waters Revival Books.

Day 44 (Page 36)

Page 60, "*The Art of Divine Contentment*" published by Still Waters Revival Books.

Day 45 (Page 37)

Page 109, "*The Art of Divine Contentment*" published by Still Waters Revival Books.

Day 46 (Page 37)

Page 208, "*The Art of Divine Contentment*" published by Still Waters Revival Books.

Day 47 (Page 38)

Page 238, *"The Art of Divine Contentment"* published by Still Waters Revival Books.

Day 48 (Page 38)

Page 244, *"The Art of Divine Contentment"* published by Still Waters Revival Books.

Day 49 (Page 39)

Page 173, *"The Reformed Pastor,"* published by Soli Deo Gloria Publications.

Day 50 (Page 39)

Page 291, *"The Saints Everlasting Rest,"* published by Soli Deo Gloria Publications.

Day 51 (Page 40)

Page 293, *"The Saints Everlasting Rest,"* published by Soli Deo Gloria Publications.

Day 52 (Page 40)

Page 374, *"The Saints Everlasting Rest,"* published by Soli Deo Gloria Publications.

Day 53 (Page 41)

Page 410, *"The Saints Everlasting Rest,"* published by Soli Deo Gloria Publications.

Day 54 (Page 41)

Page 40, *"Exercises for the Closet, for Every Day in the Year, Volume II,"* published by Ezra Collier, New York, 1838.

Day 55 (Page 42)

Page 39, *"Exercises for the Closet, for Every Day in the Year, Volume II,"* published by Ezra Collier, New York, 1838.

Day 56 (Page 42)

Page 40, *"Exercises for the Closet, for Every Day in the Year, Volume II,"* published by Ezra Collier, New York, 1838.

Day 57 (Page 43)

Page 174, "*Exercises for the Closet, for Every Day in the Year, Volume II*," published by Ezra Collier, New York, 1838.

Day 58 (Page 43)

Page 274, "*Exercises for the Closet, for Every Day in the Year, Volume II*," published by Ezra Collier, New York, 1838.

Day 59 (Page 44)

Page 311, "*Exercises for the Closet, for Every Day in the Year, Volume II*," published by Ezra Collier, New York, 1838.

Day 60 (Page 44)

Page 158, "*The Heavenly Footman*," published by Halifax, Milner and Sowerby, 1859.

Day 61 (Page 45)

Page 159, "*The Heavenly Footman,*" published by Halifax, Milner and Sowerby, 1859.

Day 62 (Page 45)

Page 161, "*The Heavenly Footman*," published by Halifax, Milner and Sowerby, 1859.

Day 63 (Page 46)

Page 186, "*The Heavenly Footman,*" published by Halifax, Milner and Sowerby, 1859.

Day 64 (Page 46)

Page 192, "*The Heavenly Footman*," published by Halifax, Milner and Sowerby, 1859.

Day 65 (Page 47)

Page 17, "*The Early Labor and Last Remains that will meet the public eye; In Several Practical Discourses*," published in Edinburgh, by J. Pillans and Sons, Parliament Square, 1800.

Day 66 (Page 47)

Page 18, "*The Early Labor and Last Remains that will meet the public eye; In Several Practical Discourses,*"published in Edinburgh, by J. Pillans and Sons, Parliament Square, 1800.

Day 67 (Page 48)

Page 18, "*The Early Labor and Last Remains that will meet the public eye; In Several Practical Discourses,*"published in Edinburgh, by J. Pillans and Sons, Parliament Square, 1800.

Day 68 (Page 48)

Page 19, "*The Early Labor and Last Remains that will meet the public eye; In Several Practical Discourses,*" published in Edinburgh, by J. Pillans and Sons, Parliament Square, 1800.

Day 69 (Page 49)

Page 112, "*The Early Labor and Last Remains that will meet the public eye; In Several Practical Discourses,*" published in Edinburgh, by J. Pillans and Sons, Parliament Square, 1800.

Day 70 (Page 49)

Page 113, "*The Early Labor and Last Remains that will meet the public eye; In Several Practical Discourses,*" published in Edinburgh, by J. Pillans and Sons, Parliament Square, 1800.

Day 71 (Page 50)

Page 250, "*The Early Labor and Last Remains that will meet the public eye; In Several Practical Discourses,*" published in Edinburgh, by J. Pillans and Sons, Parliament Square, 1800.

Day 72 (Page 50)

Page 258, "*The Early Labor and Last Remains that will meet the public eye; In Several Practical Discourses,*" published in Edinburgh, by J. Pillans and Sons, Parliament Square, 1800.

Day 73 (Page 51)

Page 330, "*The Early Labor and Last Remains that will meet the public eye; In Several Practical Discourses,*" published in Edinburgh, by J. Pillans and Sons, Parliament Square, 1800.

Day 74 (Page 51)

Page 1, "*Revival,*" published by Chapel Library.

Day 75 (Page 52)

Page 2, *"Revival,*" published by Chapel Library.

Day 76 (Page 52)

Page 5, "*Revival,*" published by Chapel Library.

Day 77 (Page 53)

Page 10, "*Revival,*" published by Chapel Library.

Day 78 (Page 53)

Page 13, "*Revival,* "published by Chapel Library.

Day 79 (Page 54)

Page 17, "*Revival,*" published by Chapel Library.

Day 80 (Page 54)

Page 28, "*Revival,* "published by Chapel Library.

Day 81 (Page 55)

Page 143, "*The Duty of Self-Denial and Ten Other Sermons,*" published by Soli Deo Gloria Publications.

Day 82 (Page 55)

Page 148, "*The Duty of Self-Denial and Ten Other Sermons,*" published by Soli Deo Gloria Publications.

Day 83 (Page 56)

Page 187, "*The Duty of Self-Denial and Ten Other Sermons*," published by Soli Deo Gloria Publications.

Day 84 (Page 56)

Page 197, "*The Duty of Self-Denial and Ten Other Sermons*," published by Soli Deo Gloria Publications.

Day 85 (Page 57)

Page 106, "*The Bruised Reed*," published by Banner of Truth Trust.

Day 86 (Page 57)

Page 116, "*The Works of John Wesley - Sermons, volume 5 - 6*," published by Baker Books.

Day 87 (Page 58)

Page 486, "*The Works of John Wesley - Sermons, volume 5 - 6*," published by Baker Books.

Day 88 (Page 58)

Page 29, "*The Works of John Wesley - Sermons, volume 5 - 6*," published by Baker Books.

Day 89 (Page 59)

Page 29, "*The Works of John Wesley - Sermons, volume 5 - 6*," published by Baker Books.

Day 90 (Page 59)

Page 36, "*The Works of John Wesley - Sermons, volume 5 - 6*," published by Baker Books.

For More Titles by *The Legacy of Home Press,*
please visit us at:

http://thelegacyofhomepress.blogspot.com

Made in the USA
San Bernardino, CA
01 February 2014